woodwind instruments repertoires

HITOMI KANEKO

THE LAYERS OF TIME IV - percolation/integration-

for Oboe and Clarinet

金子 仁美

時の層 Ⅳ～透過・合成～

オーボエとクラリネットのための

zen-on music

THE LAYERS OF TIME IV -percolation/integration- for Oboe and Clarinet

This is the fourth work of the series of *The Layers of Time*, which is written for the oboe and the clarinet. The oboe and clarinet belong to the same category of woodwind instrument and look alike each other. But there is the defining difference between them; the oboe is a double reed instrument and the clarinet is a single reed instrument.

In the layers of time, which is a main idea of this series, the two instruments emphasize their respective characteristics, and, at the same time, one percolates into the other. In addition, both of them produce new tone colors and rhythm by mixing each other.

Autumn in Paris, 2012
Hitomi Kaneko

Commissioned by Zen-On Music Company Ltd.
The world premiere : December 2, 2011, at Tsuda Hall (Tokyo)
　　　　　　The 18th annual concert of "Groupe des Quatre et ses ami(e)" organized by Zen-On
　　　　　　Fusako Nampo (Oboe) and Takashi Yamane (Clarinet)
Duration : approximately 10 minutes 30 seconds

時の層 IV 〜透過・合成〜 オーボエとクラリネットのための

「時の層」第4作目となるこの作品では、同族楽器で視覚的には似た形状でありながら、ダブルリードとシングルリードという決定的違いを持つオーボエとクラリネットを取り上げる。「時の層」シリーズのテーマである時間軸という層の中で、この二つの楽器はそれぞれの特徴を強調するとともに、一方が他方に透過し、あるいは二楽器が混じり合うことにより新たな音色やリズムを合成する。

2012年秋、パリにて
金子仁美

委嘱：全音楽譜出版社
初演：2011年12月2日、津田ホール（東京）
　　　第18回「四人組とその仲間たち」コンサート（全音楽譜出版社 主催）
　　　南方総子（オーボエ）、山根孝司（クラリネット）
演奏所要時間：約10分30秒

NOTATION

臨時記号は各小節内有効／Accidentals are effective within a measure.

♯	：1/4音高く／1/4 tone higher
♯♯	：3/4音高く／3/4 tone higher
∅	：できる限り弱く／as quiet as possible
(beamed notes symbol)	：できる限り速く／as fast as possible
flatt. (symbol)	：できる限り細かく／as quickly as possible
○ ● ○ ●	：同じピッチで音色を変える（○＝明、●＝暗） change the tone color in the same pitch (○ = bright, ● = dark)
(glissando symbol)	：glissando

THE LAYERS OF TIME IV
-percolation/integration-
for Oboe and Clarinet

Hitomi KANEKO

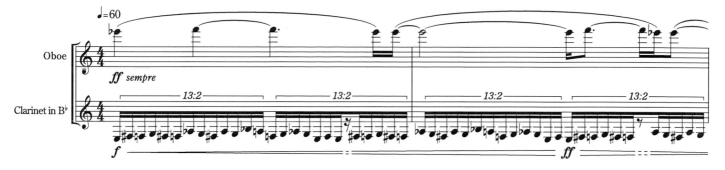

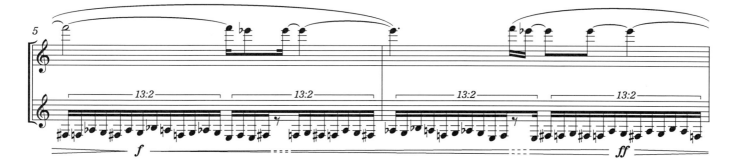

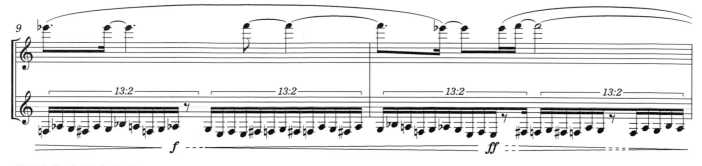

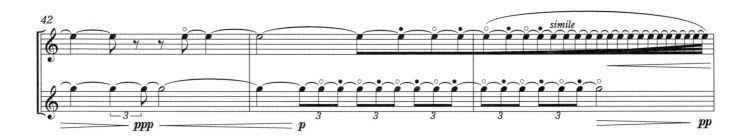

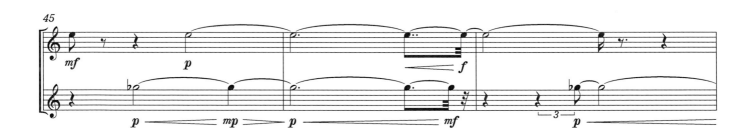

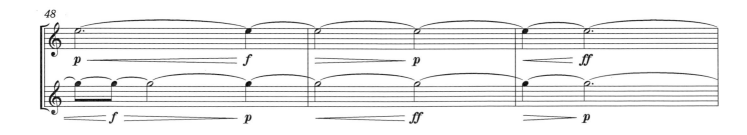

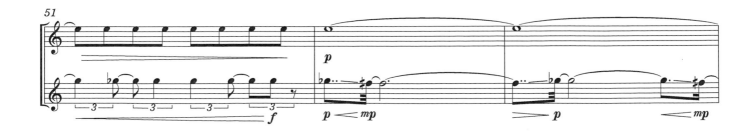

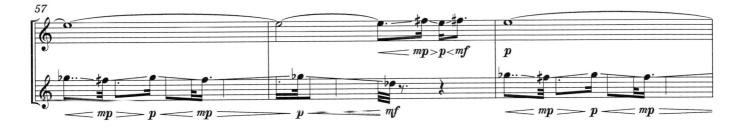

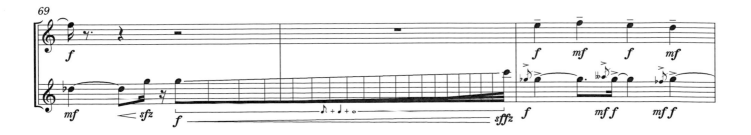

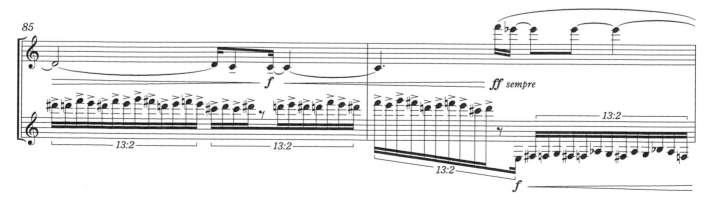

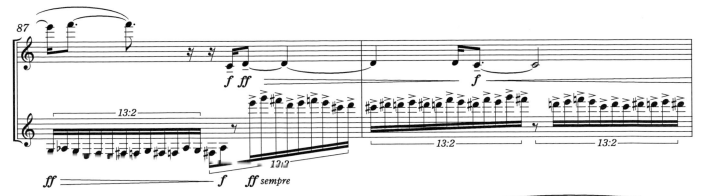

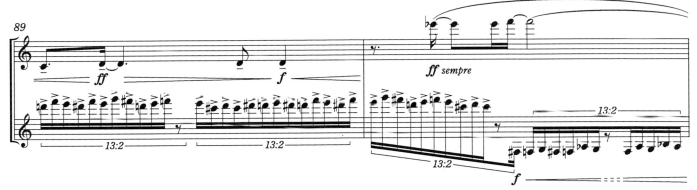

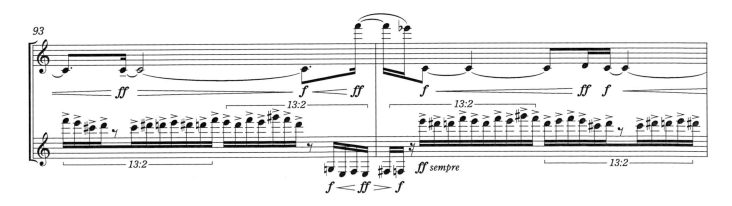

10

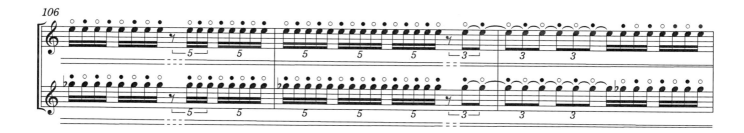

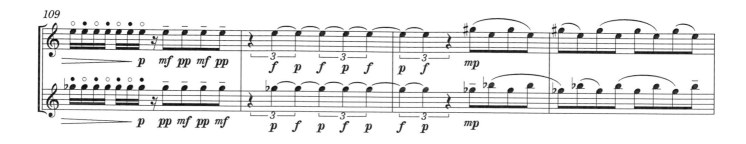

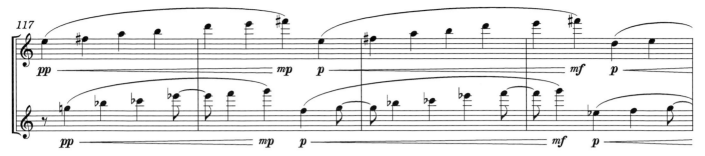

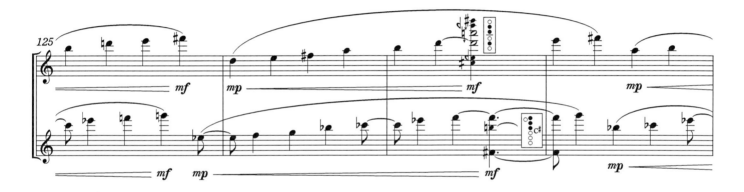

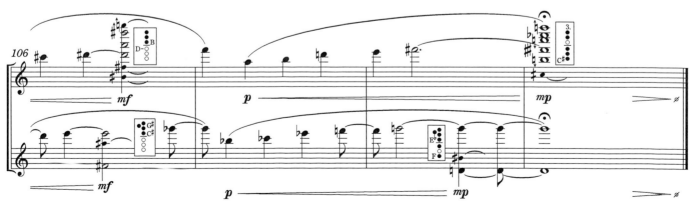

金子仁美：時の層 IV 〜透過・合成〜

作曲————————————————————金子仁美
第1版第1刷発行————————————2012年11月15日
発行————————————————————株式会社全音楽譜出版社
————————————————————東京都新宿区上落合2丁目13番3号 〒161-0034
————————————————————TEL・営業部 03・3227-6270
————————————————————出版部 03・3227-6280
————————————————————URL http://www.zen-on.co.jp/
————————————————————ISBN978-4-11-509518-2

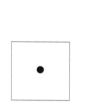

12110124